Irish High Crosses

Roger Stalley

Country House, Dublin

Published in 1996 by
Town House and Country House
Trinity House
Charleston Road
Ranelagh, Dublin 6
Ireland

Reprinted 2000

British Library Cataloguing in Publication Data. A catalogue record for this book is available from the British Library.

ISBN 0–946172–56–0

Acknowledgements
The author and publisher would like to thank the following for permission to reproduce photographs: Commissioners of Public Works (Ireland) (Photos 2, 5, 13, 20, 21, Plate 4); Jarrold Printing (Norwich) (Plates 1, 3c, 15, 16b); Historic Monuments and Buildings Branch, Department of the Environment for Northern Ireland (Crown Copyright) (Plate 3b); Minneapolis Institute of Arts (Photo 6); Trinity College, Dublin (Photo 1); Tessa Garton (Plate 16a); G F Mitchell for the photographs taken by Miss Dunlop (Plates 3a, 8, 12). All other photographs are by the author
 The author is grateful for the help received from Mary Ann Gelly, Dr Sue McNab and Dr Terry Barry. He would also like to thank Brendan Dempsey, Trinity College, who processed his black and white prints.

Cover: *Muiredach's cross at Monasterboice, Co. Louth*

Typesetting: Red Barn Publishing, Skibbereen
Printed in Spain by Estudios Gráficos Zure S.A.

CONTENTS

Figure 1
Sites with well-preserved high crosses accessible to the public.

INTRODUCTION

The freestanding crosses which embellish the ancient monasteries of Ireland are among the most attractive and skilful pieces of sculpture to survive from the so-called 'Dark Ages', a time when the art of stone carving was not widely practised on the continent of Europe. Remnants of well over two hundred crosses remain (an exact figure is hard to establish), and these probably represent less than half the number that once existed. A few are exceptionally large: those at Arboe (Co Tyrone), Moone (Co Kildare) and Monasterboice (Co Louth) reach a height of six or seven metres (Pl 1, Photo 1).

It is not uncommon to find several high crosses at the same site, though in these cases the designs are rarely repeated. The construction of the crosses involved a series of arduous tasks: quarrying the stone, shifting the blocks to the site, carving the panels and assembling the various pieces, all operations which it is easy to take for granted in our modern technological age.

Although studied for over a century (Photo 1), many aspects of the crosses are still poorly understood. Standing before the monuments at Clonmacnois (Co Offaly), Kells (Co Meath) or Monasterboice, with their bewildering range of scenes, it is tempting to assume that the experts have all the answers; but this is not so. Among the many subjects that remain a mystery are the macabre headless corpse depicted at Ahenny, Co Tipperary, and the curious scenes on the sides of the cross of the scriptures at Clonmacnois (Pl 14a). There is much debate about when the crosses were made, and nobody can be certain what models the sculptors had in front of them as they carved. The confidence and technical skill of the carving has surprised many observers, to the extent that one nineteenth-century writer was misled into thinking that the crosses were carved by Italians, or brought over the Alps from Italy!

THE FORM AND SHAPE OF THE CROSSES

Before looking at the crosses in detail, it is important to consider their structure and general form. Muiredach's cross at Monasterboice (Photos 2 & 3), so-called

5

Photo 1 *The west cross at Monasterboice, Co Louth, as illustrated in Henry O'Neill's book on Irish crosses (1857). O'Neill was one of the first antiquarians to make a serious study of the high crosses. As a passionate nationalist, he believed they demonstrated the advanced level of Irish civilisation in the early middle ages.*

because of the name recorded in an inscription on the west face, has a number of typical features. It consists of three separate pieces of stone, one of which is a massive rectangular block which serves as the base. This has sloping sides and there is a recess or step near the top. The second block, an enormous piece of sandstone weighing several tons, comprises the shaft and ringed cross head, which fits into a socket at the top of the base. The ring is the most distinctive feature of the Irish crosses, though it is not found on all of them. At the junction of the arms, the angles are softened by arcs to produce a more elegant line, and within the arcs (or 'armpits') are small rolls, features which are sometimes transferred to the inner surface of the ring. At the top of the cross is a cap, which, at Monasterboice, is made from a third, smaller piece of stone. This takes the form of a miniature house or shrine, with its own sloping roof (Photo 11). The taller crosses employ an extra piece of stone for the shaft, which required a joint below the ring. On the south cross at Castledermot, Co Kildare (Pl 2), a break in the stone at this point allows us to glimpse the mortice and tenon system used to link the stones.

Although some of the crosses are well preserved, many have suffered damage over the centuries, with crucial components being lost. In a few cases, crosses have been incorrectly reconstructed, as at Tuam (Co Galway), Clogher (Co Tyrone) and Clones (Co Monaghan), where the heads clearly do not belong to the shafts below (Photos 4 & 19). There are plenty of sites where all that is left of the original cross is a solitary base with an empty (and usually water-filled) socket. In recent years, the dangers presented by atmospheric pollution have encouraged the authorities to move a number of crosses indoors for protection; this includes crosses at Cashel (Co Tipperary), Moone, Clonmacnois and Tuam.

The ringed cross is, in visual terms, a satisfying form and the shape is usually emphasised by the roll mouldings which reinforce the outline. But, however pleasing the design, some features of the crosses are not easy to explain. The base is often larger than necessary to serve merely as a support, and the purpose of the ring and capstone has engendered much debate.

Some authorities believe the design evolved over several centuries, with very little influence from abroad, as Irish craftsmen gradually mastered the art of stone carving. By AD 700, if not a century before, standing stones had already appeared,

Photo 2
Muiredach's cross at Monasterboice, Co Louth. The shaft and cross head are cut from a single block of quartzy sandstone.

inscribed with crosses or other Christian symbols. At Reask, Co Kerry, a roughly-hewn stone is decorated with a cross and traditional Celtic spirals, plus the letters 'DNE', standing for *Domini,* the Latin for 'O Lord'. At Kilnasaggart, Co Armagh, a more smoothly dressed slab is engraved with a Latin cross and the name of 'Ternoc', the priest who died in 714 or 716 (Pl 3b). As the designs on these 'pillar' stones are etched on the surface rather than carved in depth, there is a huge technical gulf between them and the later high crosses. It is difficult to believe that the ringed cross evolved from them directly.

Other scholars are convinced that the rings were introduced as a technical feature to provide structural support. If the arms of a stone cross remain unsupported, there is always the danger of them sheering off under their own weight. The lower sections of the ring, it is argued, provide useful reinforcement. But this theory fails to take into account the symbolic connotations of the ring.

The idea of a cross in a circle had a long history before it reached Ireland. In the fourth and fifth centuries AD the motif was already being used by the Romans on carved ivories and sculptured sarcophagi. The circle was usually designed as a wreath, an ancient symbol of triumph, to underline the fact that Christ's suffering on the cross led to victory over death. Sometimes the wreath consisted of fruit and flowers, representing rebirth and renewal. In these early designs it was normal for the cross to be completely enclosed within the circular frame, but a linen hanging from Egypt (*c.* AD 500) shows an arrangement that foreshadows the design of the Irish crosses (Photo 6). The ringed cross was thus a symbolic form known to the early Christians and familiar to the Irish monks. The circular

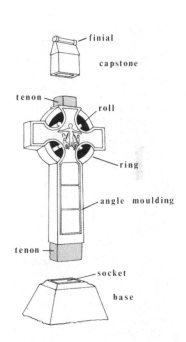

finial
capstone
tenon
roll
ring
angle moulding
tenon
socket
base

Photo 3 *Diagram showing the chief components of Muiredach's cross at Monasterboice, Co Louth.*

9

Photo 4 *Crosses at Clogher, Co Tyrone, where ornamental panels are combined with plain surfaces.*

form may also have suggested thoughts of the cosmos, demonstrating that Christ's powers extended to all parts of the world.

The cross depicted on the Egyptian textile has another intriguing feature. It is fixed into a base which has a slot at the top and offsets at the sides, features later repeated on the Irish crosses. The design is thought to have derived from the famous cross erected as a memorial on the rock of Golgotha, where Christ himself had died. According to pilgrims who visited Jerusalem, the rock of Golgotha was

cut into a narrow block, with a slot at the top for the cross. It is difficult to avoid the conclusion that the heavy bases of the Irish crosses were intended, at least in origin, to recall the rock of Calvary.

CONSTRUCTION OF THE CROSSES

Modern sculptors have pointed out that the shape of the ringed cross is not one that comes naturally in stone. The mortice and tenon system of jointing is reminiscent of carpentry and the deep recesses within the ring must have been extremely awkward to cut. No doubt there were occasions when pieces of the ring inadvertently broke off and work had to begin again. It is no surprise that masons often played safe and left the ring as a solid block.

Several crosses remain unfinished, like those at Errigal Keeroge, Co Tyrone (Photo 7), and one beside the church at Kells (Photo 8). In the latter case, the areas intended for figure sculpture have been blocked out as projecting panels, and considerable progress has been made with the carving of the crucifixion. It is curious to note that the interlace patterns on the ring were finished before other parts of the decoration were begun. At Errigal Keeroge there are guide-

Photo 5 *The ringless cross at Carndonagh, Co Donegal, traditionally regarded as one of the earliest crosses, on account of the simple incised technique of carving and the presence of broad ribbon interlace. A later date, probably the ninth century, is now generally preferred.*

11

lines on the east face, but a flaw in the stone seems to have deterred the masons from going any further.

The choice of stone was obviously a crucial factor and most of the crosses are made from some type of sandstone, which is relatively easy to work. In many cases, as at Arboe and Armagh, this has weathered badly, but the hard quartzy sandstone used for Muiredach's cross at Monasterboice has survived in excellent condition. In the Barrow Valley, at Moone and Castledermot for example, the sculptors were forced to use granite and, while the colour and texture are attractive, it was extremely tough to carve (Pls 1, 2, 12 & 13). Equally robust was the hard grey carboniferous limestone used for the twelfth-century crosses in Clare and Aran. The sculptors of the earlier period seem to have avoided this stone, although it weathers well and lends itself to precise details, as can be seen at Dysert O Dea, Co Clare (Pls 15 & 16a), and Kilfenora, Co Clare (Photo 20). Whatever the stone used, a well-tempered chisel, continually sharpened, was the mason's most precious possession. When searching for suitable materials, local knowledge was essential, and there was no substitute for experience when quarrying large blocks, free of flaws. These blocks were cut from narrow horizontal beds, which meant that, when the cross was erected, the stone lay against the bedding plane. This has often led to erosion, particularly around the top surfaces of the ring.

Unfortunately, little is known about the masons themselves; about how they were trained and where they were based. It is unlikely that stone carving was a full-time occupation, though this would depend on the extent to which masons were prepared to travel. In some cases it is possible to detect the hand of the same

Photo 7 *Errigal Keeroge, Co Tyrone. One of many crosses in which the ring has not been pierced. It is possible that the carving was abandoned, perhaps because of a flaw in the stone.*

Photo 8 *The unfinished cross at Kells, Co Meath. The crucifixion is almost complete, though carving on the blocked-out panels below had not yet been started.*

craftsman at work in different places, as at Monasterboice, Clonmacnois and Durrow, Co Offaly (Pls 3a & 8, Photo 13), but all too often decay has made stylistic comparison difficult. The major sculptors must have been men of some status, a point illustrated by the exquisite tomb slab at Clonmacnois commemorating 'Thuathal saer', Thuathal the craftsman (Pl 5b).

Detailed carving was evidently done on site, close to where the cross was to be erected, with the stone lying on the ground. In order to avoid damage to faces already carved, the work must have been done on a bed of sand or soft earth. The final assembly would have called for a heavy scaffold, along with ropes, pulleys and hoists. With the cross complete, it was time for the painters to take over. Although no traces of pigment have yet been found, it is known that Anglo-Saxon crosses were painted and it would be strange if the Irish love of bright colour, so obvious in metalwork and illuminated manuscripts, was not also reflected in stone.

13

Photo 9 *The
crucifixion, as
depicted on
Muiredach's
cross at
Monasterboice,
Co Louth. Above
and below are
two examples of
snake boss
ornament,
probably
selected as a
reference to
original sin.*

DIFFERENT TYPES OF CROSS

There are many differences of design between the various crosses, which has led scholars to arrange them in groups or 'schools' according to place, type of stone, style of decoration, choice of subjects, and so on. These analyses can be quite complicated and it is easier, at least initially, to think in terms of three broad but overlapping categories: crosses which are relatively plain, those decorated principally with abstract ornament and those dominated by Christian figure sculpture.

Plain Crosses

Photo 10 *Pilate
washing his
hands, on the
end of the arm of
Muiredach's
cross at
Monasterboice,
Co Louth. The
scene on the
panel above may
be Christ's entry
into Jerusalem.*

Crosses with plain surfaces, or with relatively little ornament, form a larger group than is generally realised. In the country graveyard at Castlekeeran, Co Meath, are three such crosses, rising starkly above the undergrowth (Pl 3c). The stone is well dressed, with clearly defined angle rolls and a few isolated pieces of decoration. Not all plain crosses are as well finished as these, and in many instances they were no doubt regarded as a cheap alternative to the more ornate varieties.

Ornamental Crosses

The most famous of the ornamental crosses are the pair at Ahenny, which stand in a remote graveyard on a hillside in County Tipperary (Pls 6 & 7). These belong to a group of

14

Photo 11 *The ascension of Christ on the capstone of Muiredach's cross at Monasterboice, Co Louth. Two angels, one, curiously, holding a book, lift Christ heavenward.*

crosses in the neighbourhood which display strong regional characteristics. Ahenny is a mysterious place, as there is no historical record of a monastery there. The crosses have widely spaced rings with tight arcs at the junction of the arms. The main shaft rises well above the ring, an unusual feature, and the north cross retains a peculiar conical capstone. The sculptural relief found on both crosses is very powerful, with deep recesses and strongly projecting bosses and cable mouldings. The surfaces are covered with an array of decoration, much of it characteristic of Irish ornament of the period — interlace, Celtic spirals, geometrical patterns and (on the north cross) a set of entangled men.

Like structural rivets, the bosses coincide with major joints, which suggests that the cross was inspired by a prototype in metal or wood, perhaps a local altar cross of some renown. The choice of decorative motifs, including the cable patterns on the mouldings, can be compared with contemporary metalwork and, if painted, the analogy would have been even more striking. The inspiration of metalwork, so evident at Ahenny, reminds us of the potential influence of works in other media, such as paintings, wood carvings or textiles, virtually all of which have now been lost.

The Scripture Crosses

The sophisticated figure carving found on the scripture crosses forms the high point of early Irish sculpture and, with their panels of Christian scenes, they have been described as 'sermons in stone'. While this is a fair description, they should not be regarded as 'picture Bibles', for they do not illustrate the stories of the Bible in

15

Photo 12
The broken cross at Kells, Co Meath, which, in its original state, must have been one of the tallest crosses.

(a) The east face, with the baptism of Christ at the bottom (the two circles represent the source of the rivers Jor and Dan) and the marriage feast at Cana above. The other panels are difficult to interpret.

(b) The west face, depicting Noah's ark and Adam and Eve.

any systematic way. Rather, subjects were chosen for their spiritual or symbolical meaning, to underline fundamental aspects of the Christian faith.

If the crosses are taken together, about ninety separate subjects can be identified, but for each cross the selection was never the same. Even when individual panels are repeated, the arrangement differs. This individuality suggests that local officials had a major say in the composition, with scenes being chosen to suit the preferences of particular monasteries. Nevertheless, a number of broad themes can generally be discerned.

For Christian believers, Christ's suffering and death brought the promise of redemption, a theme emphasised by the crucifixion, which is usually located in the centre of the cross. In most cases the two soldiers, Stephaton and Longinus, are found on either side, one offering vinegar to the dying Christ, the other piercing his side with a lance (Photo 9). Scenes leading up to the crucifixion are sometimes arranged nearby: the entry into Jerusalem, for example, or the mocking of Christ. Muiredach's cross at Monasterboice has a particularly full cycle of such scenes,

16

cont. p 33

Pl 1 *The cross at Moone, Co Kildare, one of several granite crosses in this part of the country.*

17

Pl 2 *The south cross at Castledermot, Co Kildare. The crucifixion is flanked by scenes of David playing his harp (left) and Abraham about to sacrifice Isaac (right); below are St Paul and St Anthony being fed by the raven.*

18

Pl 3a *The Last Judgement as depicted on the cross at Durrow, Co Offaly. The rounded modelling of the figures is characteristic of the midland scripture crosses.*

Pl 3b *The pillar stone at Kilnasaggart, Co Armagh, engraved with a cross and an inscription referring to Ternoc the priest, who died in 714 or 716.*

Pl 3c *Castlekeeran, Co Meath, where the ancient graveyard contains three undecorated crosses, impressive in their stark simplicity.*

19

Pl 4 *The 'cross of the scriptures' at Clonmacnois, Co Offaly. The first scene above the base shows the resurrection of Christ, with two soldiers seated either side of the tomb.*

Pl 5a *The base of the cross of the scriptures at Clonmacnois, Co Offaly, showing two chariots and three horsemen. Similar subjects can be found on other crosses.*

Pl 5b *Grave slab at Clonmacnois, Co Offaly, inscribed, 'OR DO TIIUATIIAL SAER' (Pray for Thuathal the craftsman). Although usually displayed in a vertical position, the inscription was intended to be read from the side.*

Pl 6 *The north cross at Ahenny, Co Tipperary. Figure sculpture is restricted to the base, the east face of which (depicted here) shows Adam and the animals in the Garden of Eden.*

Pl 7a & b *The north cross at Ahenny, Co Tipperary, where precious metalwork appears to have inspired the carving of the spiral patterns and the cable ornament around the edges.*

23

Pl 8 *Muiredach's cross at Monasterboice, Co Louth: Christ being mocked as King of the Jews. Note the ornate brooch, indicating royal status. The inscription mentioning Muiredach is visible below.*

24

Pl 9 *The Last Judgement as depicted on Muiredach's cross at Monasterboice, Co Louth. David plays his harp to the left of Christ, and (opposite) a devil armed with a fork chases the damned into hell. Below, a soul is being weighed, while a devil sprawls beneath the scales.*

25

Pl 10 *The north cross at Castledermot, Co Kildare. Adam and Eve are placed, unusually, in the centre of the cross, while the crucifixion is on the opposite face. The four surrounding scenes are the fall of Simon Magus (top), Abraham and Isaac (right), Daniel in the lions' den (below) and David with his harp (left).*

26

Pl 11 *Old Testament scenes.*

(a) *Adam and Eve, with Cain killing Abel to the right, as depicted on Muiredach's cross at Monasterboice, Co Louth.*

(b) *Abraham about to sacrifice Isaac, with the angel and the ram in the top right corner, as shown on the cross at Durrow, Co Offaly.*

27

Pl 12 *Moone, Co Kildare: the twelve apostles and the crucifixion. The geometrical style is probably explained by the influence of metalwork.*

28

Pl 13 *Moone, Co Kildare: three Hebrews in the furnace, with (below) the flight into Egypt and a beautifully simplified version of the miracle of the loaves and fishes (with two extra eels?).*

29

Pl 14a *The north face of the cross of the scriptures at Clonmacnois, Co Offaly. Two unidentified subjects. The top scene may represent an evangelist seated on the shoulders of a prophet.*

Pl 14b *Fragmentary cross at Clonmacnois, Co Offaly. The two lions, with their jaws interlaced, are reminiscent of designs in the Book of Kells.*

30

31

Pl 16a *The cross at Dysert O Dea, Co Clare, showing three panels of animal interlace, executed in a degenerate version of the 'Irish Urnes' style. Note the extent of the relief of the ecclesiastical to the left.*

Pl 16b *Beard pullers from Muiredach's cross at Monasterboice, Co Louth.*

(Facing page) Photo 13 *The cross of the scriptures at Clonmacnois, Co Offaly. Immediately above the inscription is a scene usually interpreted as the founding of the monastery by St Ciaran and King Diarmait.*

32

cont. from p 16

though they are not arranged in chronological order. On the outer face of the north arm is the flagellation of Christ; opposite, on the south, is Pontius Pilate washing his hands (Photo 10). At the base of the shaft (west face) is a scene in which Christ is mocked as King of the Jews, a scene often mistaken for the arrest (Pl 8). The crucifixion occupies the centre of the cross and the resurrection is squashed into the right arm. Below, on the shaft, comes a scene which could be Christ's reappearance to the apostles, with doubting Thomas pointing towards Christ's wounds. Finally, on the capstone is the ascension, with Christ lifted heavenward by angels (Photo 11). The viewer has to keep moving to follow the scenes, and the biblical sequence of events was obviously not of paramount importance to the sculptors.

Christ's public life and miracles are another prominent theme. During the early Middle Ages, miracles played an important role in the spread of Christianity, particularly in the conversion of barbarian peoples in northern Europe. Many of the early saints were revered as great miracle workers. While the miracles depicted on the crosses underline the divine powers of Christ, they had an additional symbolic purpose. The two favourites, the feeding of the five thousand with the loaves and fishes (Pl 13) and the wedding feast in Cana of Galilee (Photo 12a), involved bread and wine, foreshadowing the consecration of bread and wine in the Christian eucharist.

A stress on the eucharist helps to explain the popularity of the scene depicting St Paul and St Anthony. These saints of the Egyptian desert may seem rather obscure, but they were honoured in Ireland as the fathers of monasticism. When St Anthony, who withstood all manner of fearful torments and temptations, encountered St Paul, the pair were fed by a raven bringing bread from heaven. Their breaking of bread together was a reminder of the eucharist, a point emphasised at Castledermot (south cross), where the scene is placed under the crucifixion (Pl 2).

Christ came into the world to atone for the transgressions of Adam and Eve and, as a consequence, Christian writers linked the wood of the cross to the tree in the Garden of Eden from which the forbidden fruit was taken. As the medieval theologian, Fulbert of Chartres, explained, 'Christ, the beginning, end, resurrection and life ... by hanging from a cross with a tree's help took away the poison that came from a tree, and opened again the closed doors to life'. This link is made explicit on the crosses through the depiction of Adam and Eve (Pl 11a, Photo 12b), a scene which in some cases was the first of a sequence of Old Testament subjects.

Old Testament scenes were usually selected for their 'typological' significance; in other words, for the way in which they foreshadowed events associated with Christ. Thus, Abel, who had sacrificed a lamb to God and who was slain by his brother Cain, was regarded as a 'type' or prefiguration of Christ (Pl 11a); so, too, David, who saved the Israelites from Goliath, Moses, who brought forth water from the desert, and Isaac, who was placed on the altar as a sacrificial victim by his father Abraham (Pls 10 & 11b). Sculptures of David, frequently shown with his harp, were

especially popular. As the author of the psalms, which were sung or recited almost continuously in the Irish monasteries, he was held in great esteem (Pls 2 & 10).

Some Old Testament events were selected because of their link with the theme of deliverance. Subjects of this type were among the first to appear in Christian art, in the tomb sculptures and catacombs of Rome. They relate to prayers in which God's help was requested by those in peril or in danger of death. Thus the penitent sought help, just as God had saved Noah from the flood, Isaac from his father's sword, Daniel from the lions and the three Hebrews from the furnace (Pl 13). Versions of the prayer (known as the *ordo commendationis animae*) were employed in the Irish Church, and the scenes on the crosses reflect this use.

The Last Judgement (or sometimes a vision of Christ in glory) was depicted as a counterpart to the crucifixion on the reverse face of the cross, as at Clonmacnois and Durrow (Pl 3a). The Last Judgement on Muiredach's cross is especially rich in detail (Pl 9). A demon with a three-pronged fork thrusts the damned into hell, while the elect in heaven are led by David playing his harp. Below Christ's feet are the scales of judgement, the devil spreadeagled beneath. Over his shoulders Christ holds a cross and a flowering rod, a standard formula in Ireland that is also found in illuminated manuscripts. It is a curious pose which has been traced back to pre-Christian sources in Egypt — to representations of the god Osiris.

In several of the Ulster monuments, at Arboe and Donaghmore, Co Tyrone, for example, Old and New Testament are kept apart on opposite faces of the cross, but elsewhere the arrangement is not always as logical. At Castledermot (south cross), the west face includes Christ's journey to Emmaus and the ascension, as well as such Old Testament scenes as Adam and Eve, David and his harp, and Abraham and Isaac (Pl 2). A symbolic rationale might lie behind the arrangement, but it was probably caused by the decision to concentrate the biblical scenes on one face of the cross only.

After this general survey, it is worth looking at two crosses in more detail, beginning with the granite cross at Moone (Pl 1). This elegantly proportioned monument is unusual, since the Christian scenes are concentrated on the base. The carving is famous for its flat geometrical style, in which human bodies are rendered in simple squares or rectangles (Pl 12). It has been suggested that this was

35

Photo 15
*Fragmentary
cross from
Kinnitty, Co
Offaly, now at
Castlebernard.
The badly
damaged
inscription
appears to
mention the
name of the high
king, Mael
Sechnaill, which
implies a date
for the cross of
c. 846–62.*

unavoidable, given the coarse nature of the granite, but it is more likely to be the result of copying stylised models, perhaps in metalwork. The crucifixion appears on one face and, with naïve charm, the apostles are arranged in symmetrical lines below. Christ wears the long garment or 'colobium', rather than a simple loin cloth around the waist. On the opposite side of the cross is the Fall of Man, with the snake entwined around the tree between Adam and Eve. Three panels are devoted to 'deliverance' scenes and another depicts a miracle of Christ, a wonderfully simplified version of the feeding of the five thousand, with the subject reduced to five circles (for loaves), two fishes and two non-biblical eels (Pl 13)!

At Moone the subjects are composed in a direct and recognisable way, but on the cross of the scriptures at Clonmacnois there is far less certainty about the scenes depicted (Pl 4). The west face has the usual crucifixion, the naked body of Christ modelled with expression and sensitivity. Below are two scenes which probably represent the arrest of Christ and Christ being shown to the people. Underneath is the resurrection, composed in a uniquely Irish manner. Two soldiers face each other and, behind them, the women arrive to find the empty tomb. Below is the shrouded body of Christ, with a bird, symbolising the Holy Spirit, breathing life into the corpse. It is a strange, highly condensed version of a scene which also appears at Monasterboice, Kells and Durrow. The centre of the east face contains the Last Judgement, and a scene at the base, in which two figures clutch what appears to be a staff, is traditionally thought to be King Diarmait and St Ciaran founding the monastery at Clonmacnois (Photo 13). More problematical are the narrow sides of the cross, where only King David and his musicians can be recognised with any certainty.

The meaning of the animals, horsemen and chariots on the base of the cross are equally obscure (Pl 5a). They are not biblical scenes, and some people believe they relate to Celtic mythology or events in Irish history. Similar carvings appear on the bases of other crosses — at Kells for example (Photo 14) — which indicates that they had more than local significance. It is worth noting that hunting scenes and carvings of horsemen were popular with Pictish sculptors in Scotland. The cross of the scriptures is thus an enigmatic monument, revealing the extent to which we still do not fully understand the minds and outlook of the monastic communities of the time.

THE STYLE OF THE CARVINGS

The style of the Clonmacnois workshop has a remarkable sense of assurance. The figures are modelled in deep relief, with undulating forms and plenty of attractive detail. Round, cheerful faces add to the sense of life and spontaneity. The style is sufficiently close to that on the crosses at Durrow and Monasterboice to show that the workshop travelled extensively (Pl 3a). The market cross at Kells, its surfaces decaying from its long exposure to traffic pollution, was — almost certainly — a product of the same 'school'. The carvings are best preserved at Monasterboice, particularly on the panel showing Christ as King of the Jews (Pl 8). To emphasise his royal status, Christ is bedecked with an ornate cloak and a characteristic Irish brooch. The soldiers, who wear short trousers with impeccable gatherings, have the long hair and flamboyant moustaches apparently favoured by Irish males in the early Middle Ages. The origin of this confident figure style is a mystery. Was it learnt over a long period, or copied from foreign models, or perhaps borrowed from wood carvings? Nobody knows for sure.

In contrast, the sculpture at Moone seems diagrammatic, with the figures reduced to geometrical shapes and simple outlines. Instead of the modelled surfaces of Monasterboice, the relief is flat, almost two-dimensional. This figure style is rooted in Irish tradition. In the Flight into Egypt (Pl 13), for example, the head of Joseph has a profile encountered in the Book of Kells, consisting of a powerful

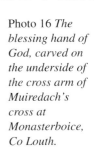

Photo 16 *The blessing hand of God, carved on the underside of the cross arm of Muiredach's cross at Monasterboice, Co Louth.*

37

jawline and hair curled at the nape of the neck. Although these contrasts in style have led to suggestions that the Moone carvings are earlier than those at Monasterboice, the choice of subjects implies that they were carved at much the same period.

Photo 17 *The twelfth-century cross at Glendalough, Co Wicklow. As at Dysert O Dea (Pl 15), an ecclesiastical figure appears below the crucifixion.*

THE DATE OF THE CROSSES

Most scholars in the past have regarded the scripture crosses at Monasterboice, Kells and Clonmacnois as the climax of a long development. Precise dates are rare, but there are a few chronological clues. The Muiredach mentioned in the inscription at Monasterboice (Pl 8) is generally thought to be the abbot who died in 923 or 924 and the cross may therefore have been carved about 900–920. But absolute certainty is not possible, for Muiredach is a common name and the inscription is an afterthought, engraved around a pair of cats. At Clonmacnois, two much defaced inscriptions on the cross of the scriptures (Photo 13) appear to mention the names of King Flann Sinna (879–916) and Abbot Colman (d. 924), which suggests a date of *c.* 900–916 for the carving. The similarity of the dates for the two crosses lends support to the view that they were carved by the same workshop. A cross from Kinnitty, Co Offaly, now at Castlebernard, has recently been ascribed to 846–862, on the basis of a reading of another fragmentary inscription (Photo 15).

Some help in dating also comes from historical sources. The monastery at Kells was founded about 804, and that at Castledermot in 812, so the crosses at these sites must belong to the ninth century at the earliest. But do any of the high crosses go back to before 800? The Ahenny crosses (Pls 6 & 7), with their spectacular repertoire of decorative motifs, have sometimes been placed as early

38

as 750, but doubt is cast on this by the technical prowess of the carving, which is every bit as accomplished as the scripture crosses. It is important to appreciate that differences in style are more likely to reflect local preferences rather than the passage of time. Whatever the precise dates, it is obvious that the second half of the ninth century was a period of considerable activity in sculpture. This was a turbulent era in Irish history, for the Viking incursions were at their worst between 830 and 870. Unlike precious chalices, reliquaries and book shrines, stone monuments were of no interest to the pagan raiders. They were a more durable investment and perhaps represent a reassertion of confidence, both in the Christian faith and in the monastic establishment.

Photo 18 *Animal interlace in the 'Irish Urnes' style on the side of the cross at Glendalough, Co Wicklow.*

THE PURPOSE OF THE CROSSES

The fact that the cross of the scriptures at Clonmacnois and the cross from Kinnitty both involved the patronage of the high kings of Ireland underlines the status of these monuments. It also raises the question of what purpose the high crosses were designed to serve. It is known that crosses, perhaps very simple examples, were used as a way of establishing the sacred precinct of a monastery, by defining the boundaries and by marking out the areas of sanctuary. This helps to explain the proliferation of crosses at the same site. An extract from a poem associated with Durrow illustrates the way that crosses were seen as part of the very identity of a monastery:

> O Cormac, beautiful thy church
> With its books and learning
> A devout city with a hundred crosses

39

Photo 19 *The market cross at Tuam, Co Galway, c. 1126–56 (now in the Church of Ireland cathedral). The dense panels of interlace are reminiscent of those found on contemporary metalwork, most notably the cross of Cong.*

Stone crosses also had a commemorative function, marking places associated with miracles or major events. The monks at Iona, for example, erected a cross on the millstone where St Columba was accustomed to rest, and an inscription on the tower cross at Kells commemorates St Columba and St Patrick. Although burials were made near high crosses, there is no evidence that they were designed as funerary monuments. Indeed, the inscriptions usually imply that the individuals recorded were still alive when the crosses were carved. The inscription at Monasterboice reads: 'OR DO MUIREDACH LAS NDERNAD I CHROSSA' (Pray for Muiredach who has caused this cross to be erected) (Pl 8). Sadly, it does not tell us why Muiredach erected the cross and whether his motives amounted to anything more than an assertion of his personal status.

There is little doubt that crosses often served as places of prayer and penance, and it is possible that specific services or liturgical ceremonies occurred beside them, particularly on Good Friday. The blessing hand stretching out under the arm of both the cross of the scriptures at Clonmacnois and Muiredach's cross at Monasterboice (Photo 16) makes sense if we imagine the faithful kneeling below. But, for prayer and worship, relatively plain crosses would have sufficed, and the complexity of the sculpture still needs to be explained.

40

Photo 20 *The 'Doorty' cross at Kilfenora, Co Clare. The ecclesiastic points to an enigmatic scene in which two figures thrust croziers into a monstrous bird below.*

41

It has often been suggested that the scripture crosses were designed for teaching, with the Christian truths being expounded to layfolk gathered around. This is perhaps too romantic a view, as the scenes are not always easy to see and comprehend. They appear better suited to an educated monastic audience than to the local populace. The distinguished scholar, Robin Flower, suggested that they may have had a semi-magical role, acting as a defence against the forces of evil, a permanent prayer to God. It is an intriguing idea, for the scripture crosses are indeed permanent and tangible statements of the Christian faith. But there were, no doubt, more prosaic considerations. It is hard to avoid the impression that ornate stone crosses, intricately carved and painted, were used by ambitious kings and monastic rulers as a way of proclaiming their own status and authority.

TWELFTH-CENTURY CROSSES

A revival of cross carving took place in the twelfth century, at a time when the Irish Church was undergoing reform. With many changes from the earlier crosses, there is not much continuity of design. The twelfth-century examples appear at new sites, rather than at the old established monasteries, and there is a heavy concentration in Munster. Many were constructed from the grey limestone ubiquitous in the west. The ringed head, when it appears, tends to be more compact, and biblical scenes are largely absent. Instead, the crucified Christ and an ecclesiastic are given great prominence, their forms often projecting in powerful relief. Sometimes they are portrayed on opposite sides of the cross, but at Dysert O Dea (Pl 15) and at Glendalough (Photo 17) they are placed one above the other. During the twelfth

42

Photo 22
Ornamental panels from Muiredach's cross at Monasterboice, Co Louth.

(a) *Eight men with entangled limbs, a theme also found in Pictish carving and in the Book of Kells.*

(b) *Vine-scrolls containing birds and beasts, a design rare in Ireland but popular in Anglo-Saxon England.*

43

century, a diocesan hierarchy of bishops was imposed on the Irish Church, and it is thought by some scholars that the crosses were designed to assert the authority of bishops.

The shafts of the crosses are usually covered in fine interlace and complicated animal patterns. The latter are designed in the so-called 'Irish-Urnes' style, in which diagonally arranged beasts are enmeshed in coils of snakes (Pl 16a, Photo 18). There are many such panels at Tuam, delicately incised in thin relief (Photo 19). In its original state, the cross at Tuam must have been an enormous monument, worthy of Turlough O Conor, King of Connacht (1106–56) and High King of Ireland, whose name is recorded on it. Turlough was responsible for commissioning the cross of Cong (1127–36), the gilded bronze processional cross in the National Museum, which has animal patterns similar to those at Tuam. With the ornament picked out in paint, the cross at Tuam must have been intended to look like a giant version of the goldsmith's work.

Several of the twelfth-century crosses had extra pieces of stone inserted, and one at Dysert O Dea (now missing) comprised the outstretched arm of the bishop. But the cross with the most unusual structure is that at Cashel, where there is no ring and the arms are so long that vertical stays were needed as support (Photo 21). The huge image of Christ filling one side is derived from a miraculous cross at Lucca in Italy, which was copied throughout Europe in the twelfth century. The fact that the authorities at Cashel rejected traditional Irish forms in order to accommodate a foreign image reflects the impact of European art on twelfth-century Ireland. Apart from the massive scale of the base, the Cashel cross has little in common with those carved two or three centuries before.

CONCLUSION

Ireland was not the only country of northern Europe to produce ornate freestanding crosses, and fine examples (including some with rings) can be found in England, Scotland and Wales. However, most of the English crosses have been reduced to battered fragments, and Ireland is fortunate that so many of its early crosses are well preserved. With their ringed heads, the Irish examples tend to form a distinctive group and, in terms of design, their general form was unusually successful, making sense from a symbolic, structural and aesthetic point of view. It is no surprise that, during the nineteenth century, this memorable form became one of the emblems of Irish nationalism, since when examples have appeared in their thousands as tombstones throughout the land.

SELECT BIBLIOGRAPHY

Crawford, H S. 1926. *Handbook of Carved Ornament from Irish Monuments of the Christian Period*. Dublin.

de Paor, L. 1955/6. 'The Limestone Crosses of Clare and Aran' in *Journal of the Galway Archaeological and Historical Society*, 26, 53–71.

1987. 'The High Cross of Tech Theille (Tihilly), Kinnitty, and related Sculpture' in *Figures from the Past*. (Ed) E Rynne. Dublin, 131–58.

Flower, R. 1954. 'Irish High Crosses' in *Journal of the Warburg and Courtauld Institutes*, 17, 87–97.

Hamlin, A. 1987. 'Crosses in Early Ireland: The Evidence from the Written Sources' in *Ireland and Insular Art, ad 500–1200*. (Ed) Michael Ryan. Dublin, 138–40.

Harbison, P. 1992. *The High Crosses of Ireland*. 3 volumes. Bonn.

1994. *Irish High Crosses with the Figure Sculptures Explained*. Drogheda.

Henry, F. 1933. *La Sculpture Irlandaise*. Paris.

1964. *Irish High Crosses*. Dublin.

1965–70. *Irish Art*. 3 volumes. London.

O'Neill, H. 1857. *Illustrations of the Most Interesting of the Sculptured Crosses of Ancient Ireland*. London.

Roe, H M. 1959. *The High Crosses of Kells*. Meath Archaeological and Historical Society.

1969. *The High Crosses of Western Ossory*. Kilkenny Archaeological Society, 2nd edition.

1981. *Monasterboice and its Monuments*. County Louth Archaeological and Historical Society.

Stalley, R A. 1990. 'European Art and the Irish High Crosses' in *Proceedings of the Royal Irish Academy*, 90C, 135–58.

46

INDEX

47